# Y is for Yellowstone

## THE STORY BEHIND THE SCENERY®

*Dedicated to the*
*young seekers and keepers*
*of all things wild and sacred...*

**by Judy Rosen & Biff Baird**
Judy Rosen began her National Park Service career at Canyon de Chelly National Monument. She has worked as a naturalist and planner in many national parks and forests. She raises two sons while working at Rocky Mountain National Park. Biff Baird earns his living as an interpretive planner, freelance writer, and exhibit designer. A father of two, he prefers hiking, mountain-biking, skiing, and scuba-diving to working.

**Illustrations by Loren Purcell**
Loren Purcell, a second-generation wildlife artist, has been drawing for 20 years. From the time he picked up a crayon at age 6, he has found his voice through art. Now working full-time as an artist and serving as illustrator for the 19th Special Forces, he and his wife jointly operate their own studio in Las Vegas, Nevada.

*Front cover: Bison graze while Old Faithful erupts. Inside front cover: Elk resting at Yellowstone.*
*Title page: This grizzly bear cub isn't saying hi to you—he's swatting at a butterfly!*

Edited by Cheri C. Madison. Book design by Stuart Martin.
Series design by K. C. DenDooven.

Third Printing, 2005

Y IS FOR YELLOWSTONE © 2000 KC PUBLICATIONS, INC.
*"The Story Behind the Scenery"; the Eagle / Flag icon on Front Cover are registered in the U.S. Patent and Trademark Office.*
LC 00-109901. ISBN 0-88714-216-8.

*From the magical mists of rivers*
*To creatures great and small,*
*May the spirit of Yellowstone lead you*
*Through meadows green to mountains tall.*

# All About Yellowstone

Imagine: a wild, wonderful world of fire and ice. Awesome powers of nature are at work right beneath your feet. Magic and mystery await around each bend in the trail. A fantasyland? No, it's Yellowstone, our country's first national park.

Yellowstone is a special place—where fountains of scalding water shoot straight to the sky; where steam rises from cracks in the earth; where the howl of the wolf pierces the thin mountain air; where buffalo, moose, deer, elk, and bear roam forests and grasslands that seem to stretch on forever.

Imagine being the first person to discover this place. What would you have thought? Would you have known that it had

the most *hydrothermal* features on earth? That wolves, buffalo, and even rivers wouldn't always have a safe place to run free? That roads would one day lead to this special land?

Come. Touch the spirit of Yellowstone.

Horace Albright, co-founder of the National Park Service, was Yellowstone's first civilian superintendent. During his time as Park Service director from 1929 to 1933, the amount of national park land doubled and historic sites were added.

***What do you mean by...?*** *If you find a word you don't understand, take a look on page 46. There's a list there that explains what some of the big words in this book mean.*

**_A_ is for the Artists**
Who capture the moods of the land.
The morning light, an evening storm
Come alive beneath their hand.

*A*

***B*** is for the **Bison**,
Rugged symbol of the West.
They make their home in Yellowstone
Where they can roam and rest.

*B*

*C* is for **Coyotes**—
Watch them chasing mice at noon.
When you're snuggled in your bed,
Hear them howling at the moon.

*C*

# Dare to discover

DNA is like the music a conductor uses to direct the orchestra. But instead of showing whether the violins play a high or low note, DNA *molecules* show whether a kid's eyes are brown or blue, whether a tree is tall or short, and whether a bear's fur is brown or black.

Like your  fingerprint, your DNA is unique. DNA testing can tell you apart from anybody else in the world by using a hair, a toenail, a drop of blood, or anything else from your body. Since every person's DNA is different, police can use DNA tests to identify criminals or to prove someone's innocent. But no one could figure out how to do the tests. Finally someone tried the process using an *enzyme* found in a tiny creature from one of Yellowstone's hot pools—and it worked!

Imagine: if something inside a tiny creature from a hot pool can make DNA testing possible, what other miracles are out there? A cure for cancer? A way to grow more food? Someday *you* might be the scientist who uncovers one of nature's secrets.

**D** is for the **DNA**
Found in every living thing—
From bugs to trees to wolves that howl,
From bears to elk to birds that sing.

**D**

# Elegant grazers

People travel from far corners of the earth to see Yellowstone's wild animals. Some of the larger animals you'll see—pronghorn, bighorn sheep, deer, elk, and moose—are *grazers*. These animals are called grazers because they graze grasses and shrubs. They don't eat meat.

Male elk, deer, and moose have antlers, of material similar to your very own bones. Can you imagine carrying around a coat rack on your head—think how heavy it would be! Luckily, these antlers are shed each winter to lighten the load for at least half a year.

Bighorn sheep, on the other hand, grow horns out of a material much like your fingernails! They grow a little more each year, laying down rings of growth like a tree. And just like a tree, you can tell how old the males are by counting the rings. (The females only grow spikes.)

Can you believe that just from plants, these animals grow big and strong and as majestic as the landscape they live in?

A moose's day appears to be one long leisurely meal. He'll graze on leaves, twigs, and water lilies, then plop down in a meadow to chew his cud.

**_E_** is for the **Elk**
Standing proud and tall.
He calls his mate by bugling
When leaves drop in the fall.

# Fire: friend or foe?

*Kaboom*! Lightning strikes a tree. A puff of smoke appears, then a tongue of orange flame. The wind comes up, and the flames jump to another tree, then another, and soon a fire is raging out of control.

Some people saw the Yellowstone fires of 1988 as a disaster. But fire is as important to forests as sunshine and rain. Fire clears out old, crowded unhealthy stands of trees. New grasses, flowers, and shrubs flourish where sunlight reaches

the ground. Many animals that couldn't find food in the deep shade of the forest now find lots to eat in newly-created meadows.

Natural landscapes are continually changed by forces like the fires that have cleansed and renewed Yellowstone's forests for many thousands of years—nature's housekeeping.

Wildflowers and fresh green grass sprang up from the ash that very next spring.

**F** is for the **Fires**
That work as nature's broom—
Clearing the old and crowded trees,
Giving new grass and flowers room.

*F*

# Glimpse the great bears

Bears in Yellowstone are neither teddies nor terrors. In fact, they are quite misunderstood. Bears are usually content to remain far from the sights and sounds of people, grazing by themselves. They eat more grasses, roots, flowers, and berries than meat or fish. During spring, summer, and fall they need to eat enough to last an entire winter of hibernation.

*Hibernation* is sort of a special kind of sleep, where everything in a bear's body slows down. But, deep in drowsiness in her winter den, the mama bear gives birth to her cubs. The little ones snuggle against their mother, then emerge with her in the spring to learn the ways of the world.

Do you like to climb and swim? So do black bears, and they're really good at both. They're fast runners, too, much faster than you. If you're in bear country, wear a bell while hiking so the bears will hear you coming and avoid you.

Did you know that the grizzly was once in danger of disappearing altogether? The early settlers in the West were afraid of them, and killed most of them. The biggest problem grizzlies face today is losing their homes—people are building roads and towns on the land they need to hunt and graze.

**G** is for the **Grizzly Bear**,
Fearsome hump behind his head.
He eats all spring and summer—
Then in winter, goes to bed.

**G**

**H** is for the **Habitat**
Where an animal lives.
Water, food, and shelter
Are the gifts that nature gives.

H

*I* is for the **Indians**.
Many tribes traveled here
Gathering plants and hunting
Bison, sheep, elk, and deer.

*I*

# *Just do it!*®
*(become a Junior Ranger, that is)...*

To become a Junior Ranger, pick up a copy of the Junior Ranger Activity Paper at any visitor center. A park ranger will review with you all the things you need to do—including taking hikes, going to programs, finding things in the park, and more. When you're done, a ranger will review your work and award your Junior Ranger patch!

***J*** is for **Junior Ranger**.
It's easy to become one.
There's things to learn and games to play.
Discovering Yellowstone is lots of fun!

**J**

**K** is for the **Killdeer** bird.
Can you hear its call?
"Kill dee, dee-dee, dee"
From spring until the fall.

K

**_L_** is for the **Lower Falls**,
Which should be on your list
Of sights to see and things to do.
Roaring waters, floating mist.

_L_

# Magma, mud pots, and more...

Magma, the molten rock that is the fiery heart of our planet, is very close to the earth's surface at Yellowstone. Beneath the ground is a unique plumbing system of stone and a pressure cooker of gases, boiling water, and steam. This combination creates some of the most amazing sights on earth—geysers, hot springs, mud pots, and fumaroles. Yellowstone has more than 10,000 *hydrothermal* features in all.

When superheated underground water rises to the surface through cracks in the bedrock, some of it bursts into the air from *geysers*. Other waters under less pressure create *hot springs* and *pools*. *Mud pots* are pools that form when acid in the water dissolves the surrounding rock.

All of Yellowstone's thermal features change constantly, like the way the flowing waters at Mammoth Hot Springs deposit dissolved limestone to create new terraces. The water is telling a story without an end, writing a new chapter in stone every day.

Steam from water that boils below the surface escapes into the air through vents called *fumaroles*.

**M** is for **Mammoth Hot Springs.**
For untold lifetimes it has grown.
Limestone in the flowing waters
Leaves a staircase made of stone.

**M**

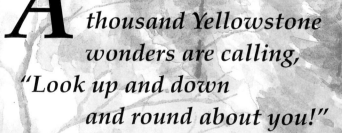

*A* thousand Yellowstone
wonders are calling,
"Look up and down
and round about you!"

—JOHN MUIR, 1898

# Nature's rarest fountains

There are fewer than 500 geysers on our planet, and more than 300 of them are in Yellowstone. Geysers are created by an extraordinary combination of underground water, heat from magma, and a plumbing system made of stone.

As heated water rises through cracks in the rock beneath the ground, it sometimes runs into a *constriction* (a place where the crack gets really small). Steam bubbles can build up below the constriction—which is like shaking up a can of soda pop, but not opening it. When the steam bubbles squeeze up through the constriction, they force the water above to overflow from the geyser. This releases a huge amount of pressure, like opening the top on that can of pop you shook up. The hot water and steam that were trapped in the cracks below the constriction explode into the air in one of nature's most spectacular displays.

As water flows from a hot spring in a runoff channel, it cools. The stream's changing colors result from the different kinds of *bacteria* and other *microorganisms* that live at different water temperatures.

*N* is for **Norris Geyser Basin**,
The hottest place in Yellowstone.
The biggest geyser in the world
Is found within this thermal zone.

N

# Out of the ordinary

John Colter of the Lewis and Clark Expedition saw the geysers of Yellowstone in 1807, and mountain man Jim Bridger explored the area about 20 years later. But when they told folks back East about the marvels they had seen, no one believed  them! It wasn't until 1871, when the paintings of Thomas Moran and the photos of William Jackson proved their existence, that the American public believed in wonders like Old Faithful.

Old Faithful is the most famous geyser in the world.

It is named for the regularity of its eruptions—which shoot water over 100 feet into the air and can last as long as 5 minutes.

In a single eruption, Old Faithful discharges enough hot water to do your family's laundry for an entire year.

*Bloop, bloop, bloop.* Bubbling blisters built up by rising gases break from a mud pot, popping one by one, like a mysterious concoction of stew.

**O** is for the **Old Faithful**
Ready? Set? Go!
A shining fountain will soon erupt–
The world's most famous geyser show.

*O*

**P** is for the **Pronghorns**
Bounding through the grass
At speeds as fast as cars can drive.
Quick—get a glimpse before they pass!

**Q** is for the **Questions**
That you can ask a ranger.
Where's the cool stuff to see?
Is there any danger?

*Q*

*R* is for the **Rivers**,
The streams and lakes and falls
That dance and sparkle in the sun
In this world without walls.

R

*S* is for the **Snow**
That can fall throughout the year.
So even in the summer
You might need your winter gear.

*S*

# The trouble with trout

Have you ever built a house of cards? If you have, you know that if you remove just one card, the whole house comes tumbling down. The balance among the plants, animals, soil, water, and air in Yellowstone is fragile, too, like a house of cards. One of the cards at the bottom is the *native* cutthroat trout.

When lake trout were introduced into Yellowstone waters, the population of native cutthroat trout dropped. At least 42 species—including eagles, pelicans, otters, and bears—depend on the cutthroat for food. Lake trout live too deep in the water for other animals to catch them. What will happen to the house if the cutthroat card is pulled away?

Fishing is very popular in Yellowstone. Just follow the rules. Keeping native cutthroat trout is limited. But you can keep as many lake trout as you can catch!

This threatened native cutthroat trout must compete with young lake trout for food—and cutthroat actually *are* food for older, larger lake trout.

**T** is for two **Trout**,
Which live in Yellowstone Lake.
Since the lake trout were introduced,
The cutthroat's future is at stake.

T

***u*** is for **Uinta Ground Squirrels.**
They spend the summer eating grass.
Then, like bears, they hibernate
Until the winter's cold has passed.

***u***

**V** is for the **Visitor Centers**
Where you can learn about the park—
Exhibits, movies, books to read,
And campfire programs after dark.

V

# Wild, wild wolves

When the West was settled, people shot wolves because wolves killed cattle, and many settlers raised cattle. They shot wolves because wolves killed deer and other animals that people hunt. They shot wolves out of fear—but wolves almost always prefer to avoid humans. Actually, wolves are like people in a lot of ways. They like to hang out in family groups, and they work together to get things done. By cooperating, they can run down and kill animals much bigger than they are, like a moose or an elk.

Wolves were gone from Yellowstone for over 50 years. But we have learned that every animal has a role to play in nature, whether humans fear them or not. Lots of people worked hard to bring wolves back to Yellowstone, and more than 100 now roam free in the park.

The wolf restoration program in Yellowstone has returned wolves to their native home in the park, where this symbol of the Wild West truly hunts wild once again.

**W** is for the **Wolves**
Running free in packs.
Though you may hear their thrilling howl,
You'll probably see only their tracks.

# Marks the SPOT!

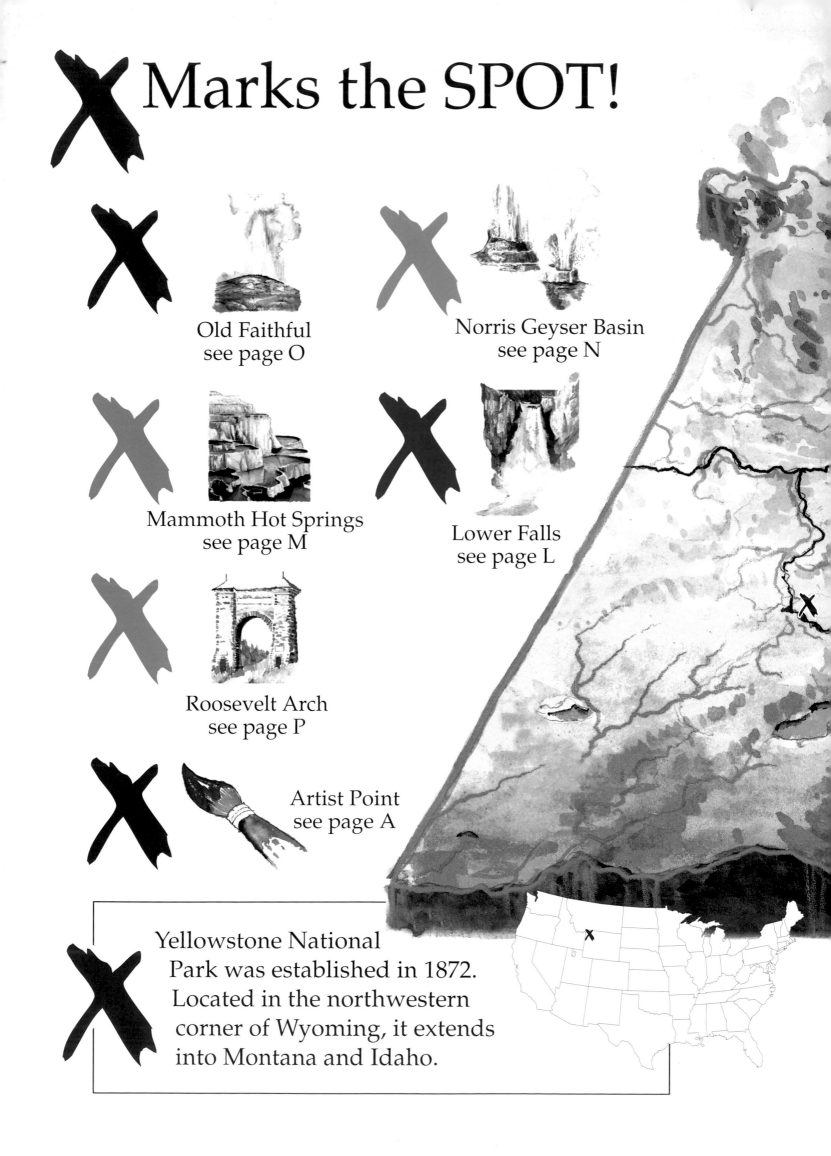

Old Faithful
see page O

Norris Geyser Basin
see page N

Mammoth Hot Springs
see page M

Lower Falls
see page L

Roosevelt Arch
see page P

Artist Point
see page A

Yellowstone National Park was established in 1872. Located in the northwestern corner of Wyoming, it extends into Montana and Idaho.

# Xtra FUN things to DO and SEE

## Yellowstone by Night
Wouldn't you love to go exploring in the dark past your bedtime? Why not get a front-row seat to Old Faithful and watch the geyser explode into the starry sky?

## Go Fishing
Catch and keep only two cutthroat trout, but as many lake trout as you wish. In fact, the more lake trout you catch, the better off the cutthroat trout will be. Remember—you need a license to fish!

## Wild, Wild Winter
Wander through Yellowstone in winter, its quietest months. Not only will there be fewer people, but it will be so cool to watch wildlife hang out by the hot springs heating themselves through this long frosty season.

X marks the spot
Where you can make your mark
Of all the places you enjoyed
In Yellowstone National Park.

# Yellowstone National Park

Legend has it that more than a century ago, a group of early explorers sat around a crackling campfire in the remote, rugged land that would become Yellowstone National Park. They talked about the wonders all around them.

They talked about protecting the land of fire and ice, and an idea was born—that there were places in the world too special for just one person to own. Places that should be protected "for all people to enjoy." Places that should be national parks.

This national park idea, an idea that began with the natural beauty and power of Yellowstone, is an idea that has spread around the world. An idea that has protected a treasure chest of special places for all of the planet's people.

It all started at Yellowstone. Now you can see why.

*Y* is for **Yellowstone**,
The first park in the nation.
Nature's beauty at its best—
Come join the celebration!

*Y*

# Zillions of things we missed

There's way more things to do and see in Yellowstone than we could get in just one book. To help pick an activity, or decide which sites to see, go to any ranger station or visitor center. You'll be able to find out about rules, pick up permits, and learn how to have a safe trip while you're there.

Here's a few of the things we missed. Zoom in for a good time!

There's more than 200 kinds of birds in the park, and hundreds of different kinds of wildflowers, and thousands of different kinds of bugs.

You can see the constellations in the night sky much better than you can from a city.

You can get a different view of the park by taking a stagecoach ride or a boat ride.

There are more than 2,000 campsites you can drive to, and hundreds more that can be reached on foot.

Yellowstone has a petrified forest. *And a whole lot more!*

**Z** is for **Zooming in**
On everything we've missed.
The things to see in Yellowstone
Make far too long a list.

Z

# What do you mean by . . . ?

*algae* (al' jē)—tiny plants; most kinds, like ordinary pond scum or the algae that can survive in Yellowstone's hot pools, live in water.

*bacteria* (bak tēr' ē ə)—tiny animals that live just about everywhere, from air to dirt to snow to hot springs to our bodies; there are millions of different kinds.

*bioprospecting* (bī' ō pros'pekt iñg)—searching for algae, bacteria, enzymes, or other living things that might be useful to humans for making things like medicines; the enzyme found at Yellowstone that makes DNA testing possible is an example of something that might be found by bioprospecting.

*endangered* (en dān'jərd)—an animal or plant species that is in danger of becoming *extinct*; the U.S. Fish and Wildlife Service makes a list of endangered species.

*enzymes* (en'zīms)—chemicals found in living things that make stuff happen; enzymes in your stomach digest your food, and enzymes in yeast make bread rise.

*extinction* (ik stiñgk'sh ən)—what happens when every single individual animal or plant of a species has died; extinction is forever.

*fumaroles* (fyōō'mərōls)—smoke holes or wanna-be hot springs. Since they don't have enough water to become hot springs, they *vent* (let off steam).

*geysers* (gī'zərs)—hot springs that build up pressure, then shoot steam and scalding water high into the air. Eruptions can last from a few minutes to many hours.

*hydrothermal* (hī'drə thûr'məl)—*Hydro* means "water" and *thermal* means "hot." Yellowstone has around 10,000 "hot water" features, like geysers, mud pots, hot springs, and fumaroles.

*habitat* (hab'i tat')—animals' homes, places where they find all the things they need to live, like food, water, and shelter.

*introduced* (in'trədōōs'd)—plants or animals that humans brought to a place, the opposite of *native*.

*microorganisms* (mī'krō ô)—a teeny-tiny plant or animal, too small to be seen by the eye.

*molecules* (mol'ə kōōl's)—the small parts of stuff; they're what you would wind up with if you had a magic tool to take stuff completely apart.

*mud pots* (mud pots)—pools of thick mud that bubble and splatter. The heat beneath the earth makes them do it!

*native* (nā´tiv)—plants or animals that were born in, belong to, or come from a certain place; native species are the ones that were in Yellowstone before humans started changing things.

*threatened* (thret´ᵊnd)—an animal or plant species that might become *endangered* if nothing is done to help it; threatened is one step from endangered on the lists made by the U.S. Fish and Wildlife Service that include all the plant and animal species that are in trouble.

"We gratefully give acknowledgement to several of our regular photographers whose work, appearing in our other Yellowstone books, was used as a basis for some of the illustrations. We wish to thank: Erwin & Peggy Bauer, Craig Blacklock/Larry Ulrich, Alan & Sandy Carey, Russ Finley and Jim Tallon, for permission to draw from their fine work."

# Did you know that . . .?

. . .The last big volcanic explosion that happened at Yellowstone (600,000 years ago) spewed out enough rock and ash to bury the entire state of Wyoming to a depth of 13 feet.

. . .After Yellowstone National Park was created in 1872, some people hunted wildlife and collected souvenirs illegally. So the U.S. Cavalry was brought in, and they ran the park for more than 30 years!

. . .In 1997 the park signed the nation's first *bioprospecting* agreement. It allows scientists to study tiny things living in hot pools to see if they can discover something like a new medicine.

# More books you'll enjoy!

### For Kids

*Park Ranger! A Book to Color*, by KEITH HOOFNAGLE and Dunmire. Yellowstone Association.

*Color Yellowstone*, by ERIC and JOY PRATHER. Joy Prather Publishing.

*Bears for Kids*, by JEFF FAIR. Cowles Creative Publishing.

*Wolves for Kids*, by TOM WOLPERT. Cowles Creative Publishing.

*Bison for Kids*, by TODD WILKINSON. Cowles Creative Publishing.

*Kids Discover: Yellowstone Park*, by LORRAINE HOPPING EGAN. Kids Discover Magazine.

*Getting to Know Yellowstone National Park*, by PATTY KNAPP. MI Adventure Publications.

*Geology Rocks!*, by CINDY BLOBAUM. Williamson Publishing.

*Forest Fire!*, by MARY ANN FRASER. Troll Publishing.

*Yellowstone: A Children's Guide*, by JUDY BEACH-BALTHIS, Firehole Press.

### From KC Publications

*Yellowstone: The Story Behind the Scenery*, by ROGER ANDERSON and CAROL SHIVELY ANDERSON.

*in pictures...Yellowstone: The Continuing Story*, by SANDRA C. and GEORGE B. ROBINSON.

*WildLife @ Yellowstone*, by SUE CONSOLO-MURPHY and KERRY MURPHY.

*Lewis and Clark: Voyage of Discovery*, by DAN MURPHY.

*Grand Teton: The Story Behind the Scenery*, by HUGH CRANDALL.

*in pictures...Grand Teton: The Continuing Story*, by JACKIE GILMORE.

# What Does the Future Hold?

Yellowstone—the world's first national park—has been protected for more than a hundred years. How will it look hundreds of years from now?

There will be change, because change is nature's law. Fires will create new meadows where forests once stood. Scalding waters full of dissolved rock will build new sculptures of stone.

Or a massive earthquake and volcano might destroy most living things in the park. And life would begin again, slowly.

Humans can't decide what changes nature will make in Yellowstone. But every visitor can make a difference, by doing simple things like not littering and not feeding wildlife. This magnificent park is for all people to enjoy, and all people need to help protect it. Every visitor to Yellowstone plays a part in its future. You, too, can make a difference!

For more information about Yellowstone National Park, visit **www.nps.gov/yell**

**KC Publications has been the leading publisher of colorful, interpretive books about National Park areas, public lands, Indian lands, and related subjects for over 40 years. We have 6 active series—over 135 titles—with Translation Packages in up to 8 languages for over half the areas we cover. Write, call, or visit our web site for our full-color catalog.**

Our series are:

**The Story Behind the Scenery**® – Compelling stories of over 65 National Park areas and similar Public Land areas. Some with Translation Packages.

**in pictures... The Continuing Story**® – A companion, pictorially oriented, series on America's National Parks. All titles have Translation Packages.

**For Young Adventurers**™ – Dedicated to young seekers and keepers of all things wild and sacred. Explore America's Heritage from A to Z.

**Voyage of Discovery**® – Exploration of the expansion of the western United States.

**Indian Culture and the Southwest** – All about Native Americans, past and present.

**Calendars** – For National Parks in dramatic full color, and a companion Color Your Own series, with crayons.

**To receive our full-color catalog featuring over 135 titles—Books, Calendars, Screen Scenes, Videos, Audio Tapes, and other related specialty products:**

**Call (800-626-9673), fax (702-433-3420), write to the address below, Or visit our web site at www.kcpublications.com**

**Published by KC Publications, 3245 E. Patrick Ln., Suite A, Las Vegas, NV 89120.**

**Inside back cover:**
Grand Prismatic Spring.

**Back cover:**
Wolf pup.

*Created, Designed, and Published in the U.S.A.*
Printed by Tien Wah Press (Pte.) Ltd, Singapore
Pre-Press by United Graphic Pte. Ltd